FIRE SONGS

DAVID HARSENT

Fire Songs

FABER & FABER

First published in 2014
by Faber & Faber Ltd
Bloomsbury House
74–77 Great Russell Street
London WC1B 3DA

Typeset by Faber & Faber Ltd
Printed in England by Martins the Printers, Berwick-upon-Tweed

A CIP record for this book
is available from the British Library

ISBN 978–0–571–31607–6

FSC
www.fsc.org
MIX
Paper from
responsible sources
FSC® C101712

2 4 6 8 10 9 7 5 3 1

To Harrison Birtwistle

When the moment came he brushed her hand away. There was light
through an open door, soft yellow surge that broke
at the foot of the bed. Someone laughed outside in the street.

How was it possible to feel them: black bacilli tumbling in the blood?
His bones outweighed him. Suddenly he could remember everything,
the house of women, the apostle window, the weather in the wood.

Contents

FIRE SONGS

Fire: *a song for Mistress Askew*

. . . fythynesse, rust, menstrue, swylle, mannys durt, adders egges,
the brede of lyes . . .
               — JOHAN BALE

The firebug rises whistling from the fire. Slats laid
on the overlap, branches at a pitch, as for Anne Askew
wordless under torture, so broken the hangman's crew
carried her to the stake, a seat where she sat astride.

It has come to this. Bramble and thorn,
lumber and junk. Dead stuff. Whatever would burn.

    *

Charge and denial; the bald accounts of martyrdom;
the mechanics at work, their gift of transformation.
Torchlight and iron. She stripped to her shift
unbidden and climbed up to the machine; when it took hold
she was lifted clear of the bed, her body hard strung,
the wrench and crack of greenstick.
                        NOTEBOOK: *She bell'd*
but speke no worde and sylence alwayes her gift.

    *

The frame of her in the fire, black to the bone. Her head
a smoking cinder, smiling, smiling, smiling.
Some stood close enough to catch the haul
and roar of flame in the summer wind as it fed,
close enough to hear the shrivel-hiss
of burning hair, to see her sag and slump, to witness
the pucker and slide of her skin, the blister-rash on her eyeballs.

In the fire lies your salvation, Anne, they said. What greater thing
than the brush of His hand as He stoops to take up your soul?

*

NOTEBOOK: *(Her Newgate poem)* –
A woman poore and blinde:
more enmyes now I have than hairs upon my hedd.

(She stood her ground.)

Then the byshopp sayd, I shuld be brente.

*

Anne, you are nothing to me. Only that you knew best
how to unfasten your gown while they waited at the rack.
Only that *she was hard prest*
which I can't now shake from my mind. Only that black
flux flowed from you, that they let you void and bleed.

*

I set this fire in a hard frost: early evening, the garden's
winter leavings, the unretrievable, the piecemeal burdens.
Paraffin to start it – that dry *whoomph!* – and I saw her ghost
chained there: the woodcut from Foxe's 'Actes
and Monuments' that hung on the chapel wall
beside 'The Light of the World', a mild-mannered Christ,
his jaunty crown of thorns . . . The minister's stage-effects
were rage and unforgiveness, his colours red and red again
which were heart's-blood and hell-fire, the least of us already lost.

*

[4]

NOTEBOOK: *(Johan Bale, her apologist)* –
By the fore heades understande she the hartes
or myndes of men. (And then): Christ wuld speake
in darke symylytudes. (And of her judges): They brede
cockatrice egges and weve the spyders webbe.

*

That they gave her cripple-water; that she ate
spoiled meat; that this was her penance; that she saw
those long nights through bedded on stone and straw;
that women in the garden by the White Tower,
turned to one another, amazed: *'What is that animal?'*
The river beat,
hour after hour as they racked her, back from the water-gate.

*

That job taken in hand by Wriothesley and Richard Rich.
Then the pyre at Smithfield; those there to watch:
Norfolk, Bonner, Bowes, priests, judges, one and all
the Devil's dishwashers. Before they lit the stack,
Shaxton preached repentance. Broken, she listened.
The crowd stood round in a ring, ten deep, and felt the scorch.

*

NOTEBOOK: *(Johan Bale, in sorrow)* –
So had Anne Askewe the flamynge brandes of fyre,
nor scremed until the first flaym reched her brest.

*

My dream of her puts me in close-by: her poor bare
feet, her shift just catching a flame that chases the line of the hem . . .
And when I wake in sunlight, that flare is the flare
in her eye, that rising note in my ear the singing deep in green
branches, that low rumble her blood at a rolling boil;
and what she screams from the centre, now, as her hair
goes up in a rush, as her fingers char,
as the spit on her tongue bubbles and froths, as she browns from heel
to head, as she cracks and splits, as she renders to spoil:
the only thing she can get to me through the furnace, as I lean
in to her, is *yes, it will be fire it will be fire it will be fire* . . .

The Fool Alone

In this, the mechanic of loss. In this, the trapper's trapper. In this,
adeptus of the abyss.
His cosh is a condom that goes the whole nine yards. In this,

not flesh but fish
not fish but fowl, not foul- but fair-exchange: the last of your cash
for the right to make a wish

on his one white eye, blind eye, all-seeing eye. In this, his laugh
or puke or cough
stops you dead in your tracks, bamboozled by the rough

edge to his rannygazoo
as he matches his leer to your smile. In this, the true
lover. In this, a blue

joke and sight of his arse. Never so chipper, never so chock-a-block
with merriment, so cock-
-a-hoop, cocksure, bug-eyed with glee, the bandy lope, the clock-

work pirouette, the way
his shadow falls on yours, that all his game is shadow-play,
that in this he's popinjay

and guttersnipe, he's seer and stumblebum. There's a thin
line you'll find between
trick and treat as you make your second guess. In this, himself alone.

Bowland Beth

That she made shapes in air

That she saw the world as pattern and light
moorland to bare mountain drawn by instinct

That she'd arrive at the corner of your eye
the ghost of herself going silent into the wind

That the music of her slipstream
was a whisper-drone tagged to wingtips

That weather was a kind of rapture

That her only dream was of flight forgotten
moment by moment as she dreamed it

That her low drift over heather quartering home ground
might bring anyone to tears

That she would open her prey in all innocence
there being nothing of anger or sorrow in it

That her beauty was prefigured

That her skydance went for nothing
hanging fire on plain air

That her name is meaningless
your mouth empty of it mind empty of it

That the gunshot was another sound amid birdcall
a judder if you had seen it her line of flight broken

That she went miles before she bled out

Sang the Rat

Gules three bars or a rat couchant natural the flag that flew over
Bryn Glas Towton Vale Flodden Field Ypres Monte Cassino that
still flies Rwanda Srebrenica Syria little camp follower they hear
your night-song death-song

Thin air on the roof-tree eye-glint in the cupboard clatter in the
wall-space coming in with the first hard frost that unmistakeable
chirrup

Your constant companion sang the rat

Rat-king thick inextricable tangle of tails fixed by excrement and ice
blood and ice nine in all all locked in the same broken run same
frozen thought same pall of red behind the eyes

Swam to shore as a raft of rats came indoors a tapestry a shawl a
quilt a blue-black shroud

There in the margins of your dream your father's dream his father's
his father's too first and last thousands taken from bilges and
strung up by the tail taken from dung-heap taken from cradle
and cot

Plague-bringer baby-killer sang the rat

Who fed at the breast of the newly delivered mother milky mouth
fur stiffened by birth-blood a story often told of how she was
milked as she slept

Who will leave a sinking ship it was said or a falling house or a field
aflame as the soul leaves the body at death

Who came as familiar to Philippa Flower tested as a witch entered
her vagina stayed there hidden while she was hanged

Who died in the pit one hundred in ten minutes neck-bitten shaken
and cracked the bull-terrier frenzied muzzle dripping the crowd
roaring bets were laid and lost screams harping to one long
scream as they were tossed backs broken in haloes of candle-light

Who rose and revived and flourished sang the rat

Forever in lust forever in heat the doe birthing and mating again in
the nest and again and ready again the buck tumbling the pups
to get at her again

Rapacious like us prolific like us omnivorous like us prodigal like us
unremitting like us like us a killer of its own kind

Sour and dank in darkness evolved to perfection like the shark
nothing to be done except what it is they do nothing else to be
except the slinky of dreams as a man might wake in the night and
feel that rumple under the sheet

Albino in snow black in ash rose-red to the open wound

Survivor of fire and flood survivor of the thresher of the terrier-
pack of the barn-shoot of the bow-trap the mill-trap the tunnel-
trap its blades and prongs angled to rip of urginea maritima
of salmonella and red squill mixed of arsenic and sugar and
wheatmeal mixed of hog's-lard and the brains of weasel done
to a paste of gas and press emerging then bright-eyed expecting
more ready for more

What does jack-rat dream of except to inherit the earth what are
rat-dreams ever else but that

Regent of the storm-drain of the shit-hole of the crawl-space of
the subway-tunnel of the cable-conduit of the landfill-site of the
chicken-coop of the killing-ground of the house grown over

[10]

Of your lady's chamber sang the rat

Gourmet of what's necrotic what suppurates whatever's gone to the
bad graveyard morsels and fancies scraps of what's soft in rot
drawn on to it by stench by a sinus-reaming reek by the blood-
glut in the slaughterhouse in the skinning-shed in the hog-yard

Some say the rat is harbinger of death some say the dead go into rats
some say rats can tell the stars that rats are star-born some say
that what rats know best was long since lost to us that what rats
know best are the soul's dim corners some speak of the preacher
rat the sin-eater rat the sacrificial rat of rat choirs rat penance
rat's blood in a silver cup

Fodder to otter and owl to kite and falcon to polecat and weasel to
marten and stoat to fox and man bitch-meat reckoned to be both
luscious and sweet

On the high beam pause and step pause and step rat's rafter dance
on water pipes gas pipes waste pipes tail to a figure eight head
down slip and shift slip and shift rat's pole dance hot-foot atop
the mulch rear up and drop rear up and drop rat's midden dance
in a field of burning stubble leap and run and stop and turn
leap and run and stop and turn rat's fire dance unseen unheard a
dimple in the air that becomes your sudden shudder rat's ghost-
dance

Danse macabre given time sang the rat

Slip-slop in the charnel house heads half-gone still with hair with
tendon with a livid slick of flesh lips a crust of ear somewhere
to feed somewhere to build a nest to crack bone for the marrow
to whelp in her crowning glory bright eyes staring out from the
skull

A boy lit on a rat by the cut backed off into water and weed fished
out a day later still wide-eyed a goodwife backed a rat into a
kitchen corner it leaped and bit she killed it with a pitchfork her
arm showed red that afternoon was swollen at bedtime the wife
was dead by dawn a rat-killer on hands and knees backed odds
on to break a dozen mouth running blood and froth hit some
malignancy choked till his heart gave way

Rat-call in the small hours the larder tunnelled and sacked loculus
in the soda bread a sucked egg soft droppings in a saucer of lard

Blinded rendered anosmic shorn of vibrissae put to the wheel or
the maze starved force-fed lobotomised infected suffocated
castrated trial by tumour trial by water by electrode by voltage
little spare-part rat-machine

With one bound jack was free sang the rat

Tinnitus: *August, sun beating the rooftops*

for Alain Palacci

You are walking down a road that is white with dust.
It could be a dream; it could be the dream will last,
unlike any shape or shade of love you care
to name (or find and follow if you must).

Empty, white with dust, and something stopless in the air:
the chain-stitch of cicadas; a dynamo somewhere.

*

What if the music of the spheres
were the cryptic *ne plus ultra* of human fears . . .

*

A single note drawn out
beyond imagining,
pitched for dog or rat
by a man with a single string
on a broken violin.

Easy to see that his penance
for gall is never to let
the music settle to silence.

*

Largo, allegro, con brio, glissando, crescendo,
vivace, veloce, da capo, da capo, da capo.

*

Something indelible behind your eyes:
the swift's wide wall-of-death between
the campanile of San Giovanni Battista
and balconies filled with flowers, a seamless scream
flowing behind the bird, a tiny twister
too sharp and shrill to be anything but lies.

A Dream Book

in somnis veritas

Will you lie with me, will you lie with me, will you lie –
was all he found to ask before she turned away.

They were in a place they mistook for a place
of safety: its one-way doors and two-way glass,

the voice-creep in the walls, her image, by and by,
going from room to room without hindrance or trace.

*

Wings out of cloud-light: that was their stock-in-trade,
the sound of it in the offing: feather and blood,

rapid *whap-whap* of the slipstream, something like
fire in a shifting wind. Or a seascape when light broke

on rockfall and she went to the edge as if she might shed
her skin in one slick strip if only he would turn and look.

*

Where the dead go through in their finery, where they go
among remnants of themselves, soft jostle, slow

promenade, a torrent of whispers, and leave a terrible press
on the air, suffocation to the living, no more, no less

than weight of sorrow, weight of loss,
memory as vacuum, love unpicked, what last words allow.

*

A path with seven gates and then a path through corn
under rolling clouds. They went knee-deep. The torn

bodies of hare and hen, of rat and crow;
the dog at full stretch; white eyes of the skinned doe,

her dugs wept milk; and the buzzard, then, its slow
drift onto roadkill. Storm-light on the fields at dawn.

*

In the house a room, in the room a chair. He sat and fell silent.
Then the pale executrix, subtle in grey, and no hint

of what might be said or else denied. It was a day of rain,
that much had been predicted. She knew it was right to lean in,

lean down, and give him the news. *Now thee aroint!*
But no: her lips by his ear, almost musical: 'Atone, atone.'

*

City streets before sunrise, the shape of himself in mist
as if, somehow, a shadow had been cast

that he might catch and fill, though he walked as someone might
who was holding off pain. She thought they would surely meet

turning a corner, face to face or hand to hand at last.
Just then the sun struck through and he was lost in white.

*

Deep reaches of sleep until the unforeseen
moment, like fugue, like *petit mal*, some kind of sign,

a touch from a joker's finger, to let him know what's right,
what's wrong with the dream-within-a-dream. A sudden, slight

shift in the order of things and all the past undone.
He left what was left of himself in her care that night.

*

They went to the river and dropped their clothes on the bank.
She struck out. He followed in the long, slow vee of her wake.

She could sound and surface, bringing back with her what
other lovers had dumped: hotel bill, gimcrack ring, a four-square shot

from the photo-booth. Later, they dipped their bottles and drank.
She looked at him and laughed. 'You think you're safe? You're not.'

*

Rain coming in across grassland, hard and fast in rising dusk.
She lives in his mind's eye; he has her there, all love, all risk,

and again in the dusk of daybreak as if she could be to hand,
somehow caught in the moment, that common ground

of rainfall and half-light, yes, as if she might ask
nothing more than to stay and map that hinterland.

*

In this, her fool is deaf and dumb and twirling a pink parasol. In this
he's doing a chicken-dance. He turns away and puckers up for a kiss.

He's their stalker, familiar, spy, his slippy grin is all
lipstick and green teeth. Words to the wise, or coffin-laugh, or catcall.

In this, he watches from cover, maestro of the deadfall.
He goosesteps them out of the tunnel of love and into the house of glass.

*

A rearrangement of stars, the long low intergalactic groan
of light unfolding in vastness, the pair of them pitched between

nothing and nothing else, words that could never be spoken
into such depth, the glance between them unbroken

through Godless years of reaching, until they see and are seen
in the very moment true light dies and returns, at once, as token.

*

Nothing so bright as this distance they walk into, silhouettes
in a film where the lovers abandon everything, all bets

off, the supporting cast crowding the screen, trying to guess
how it happened and why, children fearing the press

of years, wide-eyed and calling, calling . . . Nothing so crass
as the credits rolling up to a screamo version of 'No Regrets'.

*

As she walked towards him across the icefield the sky
sank, so she was held between white and white and by and by

he watched as she walked towards him through deep grey rain
then caught between form and fire as she walked towards him again

seeming naked, flowing, backed by the sun, and soon
she walked towards him, appearing just so, as if in memory.

*

She comes in as Columbina, comes in as Lady M, comes in
as the Rank Stupendous, all hips and lips and painted skin, comes in

as someone he knows he knows, comes in wearing her life-
mask, tip of the tongue, gleam of a tooth, glad eye, her shrilly laugh

knocking back off the walls . . . and there's the fine line drawn
between loved and lost. Comes in the complaisant wife.

*

The house might be known to them. Someone has drawn
a face on the wall in dampened ash and written below UNBORN.

Ash from the grate. In the kitchen a meal half-eaten, fruit
gone to mush, maggots in meat, a web of mould on bread. Too late

for whoever it was to have back what they used to own.
The mould is blue and beautiful and infinitely delicate.

*

A bee-line out to the edge, blind to all else, the sudden reach
underfoot of unseen ground; or else a parapet, the lurch

over the sill held off, but only just; and the sea where it runs
    blue-black
under the tilt of the cliff. Now music: a dream-time sound-track,

cymbals and strings and something that might be the catch
in her throat as she feels his hand on her hair, on her rump, on
    the small of her back.

            *

A town on a grid: high-roads and side-roads and alleys.
She went through, seeming real enough. It would be folly,

of course, to track her like that; best to find her reflection
in the smoked-glass windows of office-blocks: a kind of redaction,

herself as cypher, spectre of the concrete valleys,
her smile a smile of tireless contradiction.

            *

In the margins they find one other, in fault-lines,
where it's silences or half-heard music and the last light drains

from a low, cold sky to leave them dark
in one another's gaze and touchless as they sleepwalk

night-long in those narrows, then wake
to the same failing light, to moonrise, to music-in-chains.

            *

They pass each other unseen: that's commonplace.
They walk the cross-streets with a stalker's pace.

They are fervent in pursuit. They stop to listen or call.
They live with a changeless image of the real.

They are given over to errant thoughts of grace.
They go with their hands held out to nothing at all.

*

To him, the room is a cell: its iron bed, its single shelf
of unreadable books, nothing to bring or leave, nothing of himself;

to her, a place of peace and light: the caged bird on the sill
in constant song, the edge of sleep, that fine and full suspension of
    the will.

She goes to the mirror to find him looking back, but standing still
as if she might join him there, as if she might somehow bridge that
    sudden gulf.

*

Man of Secrets; Woman of Guile.
His artless mime; her willing smile.

They meet this side of an open door.
His touch is light; her touch is sure.

The door shuts on the rank-and-file.
He plays the fool; she plays the whore.

*

The world of windows: their reflections leave them dumb; the trip
made without knowing how, though it must have been in sleep

given the scent of wildflowers, the rockface, sun-through-cloud
and the near-impossible path to the top. Love is a kind of greed:

they know that and live by it, faux bridegroom and faux bride.
Light flows on the glass. Turning away, they let each other slip.

*

A white room empty of everything except themselves, the door
a seamless part of it, a window set on the blind side and the floor

somehow sketched-in. A word will go for nothing, though a cry
is a colourless compression in the air. No way of saying why

the space that lies between them seems to roll out so far
or how a different angle might set them eye to eye.

*

Moonrise over moorland: she strolls into that perfection
half-asleep. He watches from cover. Each wrong direction

is evidence of loss. Something runs through. There's salt
in the wind. She turns her back. He would like to call a halt

but the dream is no one's plaything, no one's fault.
Dewpools next morning carry the moon's infection.

*

A house on a hill is how they'll think of it. A full wind
to shake the place, nimbus cloud, slant rain even as planned.

They bolt the doors. They drop the window blinds. Their sleep
is near to death, and they lie face-on as if the dream might slip

from one head to the next . . . then wake in separate rooms and find
their own way back, downhill in the wet, crosswise against the slope.

*

They're watching a train go by, or they're on the train
looking out. They wave to one other. And, yes, they own

something of this: a dawn sky in Tiepolo blue
and blood-smudge, the view from the window, the view

from the hillside where they stand . . . except the stain
of their faces in the glass, indelible, is all that's true.

*

What she said to him then changed everything. Morning held off
from sunrise and birdsong. He heard someone cough

in a far room; a moth turned in the lamplight.
Although it was something he knew he knew, it wouldn't come right.

He got up and walked to the door. And why wouldn't she laugh
at just that moment? Why wouldn't she follow him out into the street?

*

[23]

She became a ghost in the kitchen, a ghost in the bed.
This was in her other life. It slipped. It held by a thread.

They went out. The ground beneath their feet was plush
with pine needles. They left a trail of trash

to see them back: certain small secrets, things better left unsaid.
They walked in each other's footsteps. That alone was rash.

*

The cave is starlit and it smells of sleep. She displaces
her body-shape in air. Here are those traces

of herself she left or lost: yes, these and more,
but she's held by the music in water . . . It goes to the core

this residue of sorrow, hallmark of the hidden places,
common ground where they stand outside the law.

*

Their hands collide. They turn and stare. They try
to remember what was said. They wonder why

things are as they are. They find themselves in the same
place at the same time not knowing how; and there the game

plays out: a cold, flat moon fixed in a cold, flat sky,
whatever it was that fell between dream and dream.

*

Rooms within rooms; something like a maze.
They call to each other. They stop to knock the walls.

She tries his other name. He finds her voice.
When he turns this way, she turns that: the choice

of no choice. When she walks off, he stays.
They are blind to one another. Face to face.

    *

Weather is massing on the far side of a hill, something like
a rolling sea building its bulk offshore and set to take

everything in sight. They wait for rain to heave above the crest.
They guess the tilt of the wind. They hope they'll soon be lost

in the spread of it, bruise-blue, and hope it might break
over their bare, bowed heads, a blessing on the unblessed.

    *

Go back to when she slipped the latch, to when he walked in
and climbed to her room by way of ladders and gantries, to when

he had his first full taste of the spittle off her lip,
to when they holed up – four walls and windowless, to her shape

in the mirror: a watermark, to the weight of skin on skin,
to guilt, to the scent of menses deep and ripe.

    *

In another place – but a place like this – they will find
shelter in a doorway. Sooner or later, he will take her hand

and cover it with his. She will feel the cool of stones,
heliotrope, as they fall into her palm. When she leans

against him, her eyes grey with rain, they will understand
how it works: the shape of his bones, the shape of her bones.

*

Her dreaming is missed connections, misheard echoes, signs misread,
is fragments and patchwork, is sight of herself on a road

that starts up at her back and ends a short step ahead,
with just enough air to breathe, just enough light to guide, and a dead-

weight in her hands that could be something like memory or could
be the dream itself, heavy with things unseen, unsolved, unsaid.

*

Dreamless sleep: not even a measure of the formless black
that holds him, something like void and voidance back to back

which must be what death is to the dead. A night-wind slaps
the shutters; rain comes in, sudden and sharp. Every lapsed

moment then, not fault but accident, not loss but lack,
and dark-eyed thumbelinas round his bed as he sleeps.

Leechdoms and Starcraft

Some men do say that starres will fall from heaven.
It is not the starres that fall, but fyre from the sky.

'Our signs are a full mismatch,' she said, 'even
as I predicted' – this and more in the dim

light of the station bar. *To stem*
a paine in the harte you must take both rue and rye

for a balm; this remedy is sure and proven.
So there's a ready help for love, a help for blame.

She travelled that night under the tireless eye
of the Great Bear: train wheels a muffled drum.

The Fool at Court

He wears seven colours in his coat and lies
with the Queen at night, and lies and lies and lies.

Fire: *love songs and descants*

So heap these on: letters, cuttings, poems, diaries, notebooks,
the black reports, the days of want and waste,
the double-entry records that set love alongside flaw,
everything said wrong, everything said in haste.

The pages curl; the words are borne up by the smoke . . .

    *

'Come inside me noiseless, like snow on water; the least
of yourself is all I want.'
                     NOTEBOOK: *(Malleus Maleficarum)* –
Knowe that they kiss his ars the Father of Lyes
each lewd in hir tourne and comen therbye to gref.

'I am lost in you. I know my name only when you speak it' –
this along with the rest, a fine burn, char and chaff. I stand backlit
against the blaze and featureless: proxy for the uninvited guest.

    *

The way this winter sun slants through the branches to bed
down in the fire, taking light, giving light; the way smoke rolls
low across the garden and holds among fern and dogwood; the way
flame gathers faces from snapshots; the way it spoils,
in particular, my sight of you, yes, the way it spoils and sings.

    *

Now it's quick shapes among trees, as if birds were flocking there,
grey birds and silent, flocking and lifting off. The singed leaves hiss.
the bole of the silver birch is tricked with soot. Time, perhaps,
    to confess,
though it might be just as well to settle for truth or dare

as seems to be the case in this double-portrait where someone
has come too close as if to smudge
the print, as if to disfigure it; and, though the moment has gone,
this remains: one soon to step back, the other close to the edge.

*

All this can be used or set aside: whatever arrives in sleep
or else is filched from memory: the Devil's patchwork
either way, a pattern of bafflement and sorrow, one slip
of the tongue, one half-hidden look, one whisky more or less.

There are standing shadows in the coming dark.

*

NOTEBOOK: *(Strindberg, 'To Damascus'): When I'm alone*
there's always someone else, although it's somehow myself.
I'm never myself alone. How can that be? The air thickens,
something takes shape. It can't be seen, but there it is beside me.

*

As if the moment will never quite pass
of shame and riddance, as if it might never seem strange . . .

A shovelling wind so the fire draws and drums.

'Nothing between us changes or can change.
If I were better suited to my dreams
love might have come more easily to me.'

*

Your hand raised: Not yet, not yet. This was when the sea
rose above the sea-wall and swamped the quayside houses.
Another where you smile into the sun:
this was when it rained through the glare and rained again
on the drive inland, coming hard and slant, us in our usual disguises,
the world a blur and nothing said. Another where you turn
as if called, and this was when something broke
from the hedgerow, fast and frightened, barely seen
except: 'It had my eyes', you said, meaning the fearful look
that now goes to the fire, shrivelled and lost.

NOTEBOOK:
the 'Confessio' – this will answer to sin without redemption
having no need of it: love-in-haste that will take
what it must and come to sorrow and then break clean.

＊

Frost in the air I breathe, leaf-fall under ice,
the evening star heavy and wet, clinker and ash
at the core, a ragged circle of scorch in the backyard grass.

'. . . nothing good can come of this or nothing
but good can come of this – which was it? I'm under glass.
I lie awake near-breathless: so still I can hear the sudden rush
as dawn comes in . . . '

'. . . last night a bird sang
out of nowhere: unearthly, stark; I listened, lying still, so still,
as if I slept with knives . . . '

'. . . awake and near-breathless:
under glass as dawn comes in; my pulse might surge and stall . . . '

＊

[31]

A crown of flame. The lattice shifts and drops. The letters soar
then settle: a delicate drift, all that's left of counterfeit and fear.

*

'. . . it's not only in dreams that I can go through fire . . .'

Effaced

On the night before her brother's wedding, Dorothy Wordsworth went to
bed wearing the ring with which William would marry Mary Hutchinson.
An account of this in her journal was later heavily deleted.

A life beyond the life and known to no one, peopled by ghosts
who can step up to be fleshed if you choose, or be held back,

can be dreamwork, can walk straight in, the invited guests
you welcome and fear. You speak for them, you give them what
    they lack,

you note what can't be said, you feel them out, keep track
of their night-lives, night-moves, hallways, hidden rooms,

all of which delights you, moving among them, shrouded in black,
widowed without being wed, feeding the fire, if you want to, with
    reams

of work half-done and left to grow in silence, that precious stack
curling and catching – last love, last light – as you burn whatever
    rhymes.

Tinnitus: *May, low skies and thunder*

Rough music in the lane,
the love-child lapped in blood
and safe at her breast, the pain
echoed in wood on wood,
steel on steel, as they come,
the women in their blacks,
to hound her from house and home,
bands of bitches and claques
of crones with their pots and pans,
their hooks and ladles and bowls,
to beat outside in the street,
to stand at her window and howl,
while the child takes a taste of green
milk and 'the dead of night'
is all she has of her own
and the music goes on and on.

Rat Again

And now, in your returning dream, they're swarming,
on Bishop Hatto, brown and black and neck and neck, a pack
big enough to bring him down and pick him to the bone.

Armistice

In the Peaceable Kingdom things go from bad to good
by way of a pleasant word where creatures are hand-fed

the lynx and the lamb and walk untroubled in a sunlit wood
of wild fruits and hymnal birdsong where children are led

daily to the sea of harmony and go as one head-
first to sound in boundless green where everyone is blood-

brother to someone where light is shed
hard to dispel the dark where ranks of the would-be sad

are gentled and set aside then to be cured
where blonde girls do their duty as they should

where language is trimmed to be better understood
where those who mistake the road out for the road

to recovery are helped back by a rolling barricade
of white roses and bramble where fire and flood

creep to meet and bond along the seam where food
is brought as song is brought as sleep is brought as bride

to bridegroom mother to long lost son set side by side
to music and applause where love is stalled

by pity where the crucified man steps down the sopping bud
of his heart in his outstretched hand while the dead

silence that draws out over battlefield and potter's field
is what remains of the truth of it and must be left unsaid

Fire: *end-scenes and outtakes*

Ils sont dans l'air, / Les ossements.
— GUILLEVIC

Dry bedrock, the scorch on corn and kale, the first of the last
on dreamtracks and flyways, a pilgrim-line stretching back
to jots on a long horizon, mile on mile through a pall of simple dust.

It will come to fire, so they say, despite the roar and roll
as continents calve from the icefields, as rainforests fall,
as the sea first takes the lowland then takes the rest,
fire nonetheless, fire on the skim of the sea, fire at the core.

My children's children will stand outside the law, to wreck
and break, to witness, to set fires, to fall on the weak.

*

When women howl in the streets, when husbands stand at their doors
with kitchen knives and baseball bats, when children stare down
through window-bars, when asylums empty in a shower of glass,
when Threadneedle Street is a DMZ, when men of God go on all fours,
when the least touch of a hand imprints as stain,
when the Politburo signs off, when fear is farce, when whores
walk out in holy blue . . . there's the butt-end of prophecy for sure.

When the peregrine catches the updraught, a sudden flame
kindling along its pinions; when it tips and stoops through the blaze.

*

City backstreets in nailhead rain, transports at every junction,
engines idling. The round-up lasted all night. They could take:
Clothing, one parcel. Food, a half-ration. Personal items, none.
Houses burned in the rain. The charred wood seemed to soften
then fall in on itself. Glass breaking everywhere.

[37]

They sang through the downpour. One woman had with her
     a book
that mapped the set of the stars, but nothing was given there
of how fast they were lost, or how often
they would stop to offload the dead in that breaking dawn.

A scatter from the tailgate: letters and lists thrown down.
You might guess their song wouldn't carry in such dull air.

                    *

NOTEBOOK: *(Dieter Klein)* –
. . . the plan: to go always at daybreak;
wake them and load them; ship them out . . . Their names
were of no account. Did they sleepwalk down the street?

                    *

The trucks clattered on. The wastefulness of prayer
was a hard lesson. Her book was 'Starcraft'; on the flyleaf, natal
     charts
for her children which read wrong
in all houses – no dark hand evident – and made of her a liar.
She held them close, her litany timed to the tap and tap of their
     hearts.

                    *

A walled city, where the Godless went through; this same square
piled high with trophies: which might mean treasure
might mean body-parts; and children spiked on the ramparts,
     so we're told.

As they rode down the Street of Locks and out to that red-rimmed,
    bare
landscape, the firestorm crowned above the rooftops, gold
leaf lifting and crusting, the great domes stove-in, everything rare
brought back to clinker and smudge . . . a goat's head in the smoke.

It burned for days: percussion of flame on the threshold, on
    the stair.
The priests heard it first in their sleep and died as they woke.

*

NOTEBOOK: *(Anon)*
. . . and everywhere torn down, defac'd, defil'd
or put to the torch: the sacred image of Christ Pantocrator.

*

When troops deploy at the crossroads, when they line the abyss,
when the glorious dead desert the necropolis,
when some slight smile leaves a scar, when what's guilty is what's
    to hand,
when the merciless doorstep the innocent,
when psychopaths enlist: a means to an end,
when children take to the streets,
when art tends to corruption, when animals turn
from the fire in the forest to face the fire in the cage,
when this fool is that fool's stooge,
when rape is a sweetener, when the unloved prompt the unborn,
when aerial shots reveal the macula
of turned earth, when spirochete and bacillus tumble in gutter-
    waste,

when money can buy only money, when the infill is hair and teeth,
when the ballast is bones . . . then it's much as you might have
    guessed . . .

        *

Dreamwork delivers jump-cuts: dust across the sun,
a killer-wind through the shanty, the long, slow stare
of the dying as they fade, the crackle and flare
of phosphorus, mother and child taken up as one,
the horizon ablaze, just as the fires
rolled in on the settlements, the sound, it was said,
of a train bearing down on the wretched, who left everything,
    who left
the new dead without pomp or prayer.

        *

They lock their doors behind them. They are carrying all they own.
They come, in time, to a place of walls and gates.
There's smoke in the sky from fires that can't be seen.

Years later, a bas-relief of this goes up: a shrine,
profiles fused in grief and fear; each starts
where another pauses for breath, or turns to speak, or crouches
    down
to filch the pockets of the dead: the way it was. A man
has covered his face with his hat. The stone blackens in rain.
If you look long enough, and hard, a shudder goes up the line.

        *

NOTEBOOK: *(Transcript)*
Our arms ached from the work of cutting throats; we seek
redemption, even here, as we kneel in the field of skulls, our prayer
to be unremembered, or numbered among the meek;
that the tally – our working day – be fed to the fire.

*

Water pours in and lies undrinkable. Bodies knock in the drift.
Even so, it will be fire. Floodwaters shift
earthworks and woodland, villages go under, the rumble of mud
brings carrion-eaters to the outskirts, brings them overhead,
and tides under a hard moon, never so bright,
fetch cars and beds and gable-ends, cattle gaffed
by the wire that fenced them. Even so . . . The bedtime story is fire, the fairy-tale is fire, the promise of light
to a dying man is really a promise of fire. What's left to be said?
A mother calls to her child. The dead call out to the dead.

*

NOTEBOOK: *Though rivers unload, though the seas grow higher,*
though standing rain is a day-long widening wall,
it will be fire, it will be fire, it will be fire . . .

[41]

Trickster Christ

His image on the water, then the man; they laughed to see it,
but soon fell silent. The storm died round him. The boat
settled into the calm, those aboard wide-eyed. And what
do you think I am, he asked, if not decoy, if not storm-light,
if not lure, if not dream-stock, if not black to your white?

*

Spittle and clay on the eyes of the cureless blind.
They laughed as the world returned.
They stared at each other's faces, wild and dumb.
The sudden blaze of daylight all but blinded them.

*

The stench of the grave still on him. A voice
called him by name as if he were first and last.
He came out in his shroud, laughing behind the gauze.
A seethe of worms ran on his flesh and fell
from his fingertips. A table was set for the feast.
The dead man sat down with the rest and ate his fill.

*

She stooped to touch and a jolt ran through him. She stooped
and caught the hem, finger and thumb. She stooped and left
the print of herself. An issue of blood twelve years: it stopped.
In that self-same moment he turned to her and laughed.

*

At the Pool of Bethesda, in broad daylight, a man
laughing a laugh meant for himself alone
as he walked away: half-lost in the crowd, then gone.

*

That roarer who cut himself with flint for love of pain,
who bedded down on tombs, who broke his chains
and howled and went naked, whose laughter was all delight
for the way he was, who felt the fight
go out of him with the mad stampede downhill
as if he should be speechless and shamed and meek and well.

*

The Mary of seven devils: he turned them out
from each of the seven portals; she bled and laughed and wept.
Later she walked at his side, no longer the slut
though his hand on the dip of her back was surely the start
of whatever would come to her that night as she slept.

Dive

A little deeper and she'll lose the light. At first
the surface is just touchable – shapes that might be clouds
or birds in flight . . . She sets her face to the skim

to get the last of the world she came from, some slight
sense of voices fading as she slips
from almost-day to almost-night, grey-green shading

first to blue, then more than blue, then to a blue never seen
by anyone but her, and that slow drift down now set to sever
all that she owned or wanted, all she had ever been.

Songs from the Same Earth

Silence of slow water, silence of the rose
that burdened the summer, silence of the still unopened book.

No returning to this, or to the stall and stoop
of the falcon through sunlight

as the cloud broke on a morning of nerveless drift,
you still carrying the shreds of a dream

in which a figure cut from black stood on the edge of things,
one arm raised to greet or else to warn.

Your voice and mine through the night,
something heartfelt, some account of solitude . . .

The spaces between us are delicate:
bird-tracks on ice, scentless depth of water below;

and nothing is accident: your face
in the mirror when the silvering slips, the raised arm

of the dreamscape silhouette, the tiercel that hunts
from high-rise city blocks in a slipstream of dead air.

II

You were setting out as dawn came on:
a slow, full brilliance akin to death.

You were somehow caught and held.
You couldn't trust the ground beneath your feet.

All deceit seemed artistry; all kindness, too. You stood
with arms wrapped round, head bowed,

rehearsing again the farce of love and forgetting.
You wear your victimhood like something cut to fit . . .

The house bells in the wind. Its mirrors glance at you.
Hallways grow dim in daylight. It starts

when you're thinking of something else: a thin pain
lodged below your heart, or where you understand your heart to be.

III

Who is he, knife in hand, the man of empty streets
and blind corners, the man of smiles?

How did you come by these images of him?
Could you pick him out in a crowd? Is there a solo blank

in the family album? Did he come to your wedding
with a gift of scissors and wearing a badge of hawthorn?

Is that his only voice – the one you best remember
from a time when you kept to the house always and slept

till the early darkness woke you?
Did you think he could become your makeshift friend?

No . . . But here he is, waiting by the path that takes you down
out of the light, where you've always thought to go,

where you think you might belong.
Who live there live in shadow. Go on . . . go on . . .

IV

Memory of crowcall: that was at daybreak
in deep frost, a sickle moon knife-edged,

the world around you noiseless in half-light.
Now you stand blue-lipped in that very place,

the morning bearing down on you, your hands
busy about your face, the memory fading fast.

v

What is it to open your eyes in this misremembered room,
to laugh at your first waking thought, to know

that cornflowers would shed a faint blue light
in just such a room at just such a time, to hear

voices plain from the shoreline
as you did, of course, when sun on a whitewashed wall

conjured a light-show that told its own story
and a moment of certain loss was building against the day?

Love given over to shame. The bright
echoes that come to nothing. The first and last of it.

When you go, take everything with you.
They are burning the stubble. Smoke folds into the sea.

VI

A room of mouths mouthing your name, you said;
then a cage of glass where your image became yourself;

then everything clear of colour, clear of sound:
a place where your eyes slowly whitened as you watched.

VII

A storm coming in off the skyline and you in the full of it,
the glare and roar, the crash of atoms,

and a wheel of birds in the still eye, barely turning,
like you in your strange, grave dance.

Will your life never settle round you – will you be found
dining in the dark, a place set there for the uninvited guest,

his appetite bound to bring a smudge of blood
to your silk, and a spillage of salt? Later, there'll be a wind

to wash you naked, and what the downpour left
in the garden drills, as you lick your fingertip to dip the salt.

VIII

You are here and nowhere else despite your dreaming
and there's something in the room like smother and smoke . . .

It's never been enough to lock the doors
or close the blinds in that moment just before dawn.

You draw down the worst of the past
in which you are bait, your old loves nudging and feeding.

IX

When the entire flock lifted as one;
when you began to lose the light; when the moon

tipped up on the skyline; when the river
glossed along its length; when you walked back, when you walked

that needless mile, trying to empty your mind;
when you seemed to catch night's rhythm coming in,

a long, slow, seismic pulse; when you knew
there were words you would never speak or want to hear; when rain

started up from the earth, a whisper in the grass;
when you called out, when you called

to clear the air and nothing more; when you crossed the line
that keeps what's yours from what the world holds back, then –

this bird-skull, eaten clean, eye-sockets clean,
dome and beak intact, a talisman to see you home, to watch the
    door . . .

My last sight of you will come as you pass the window,
your look-and-look-away a sudden gleam in the glass.

Tinnitus: *January, thin rain becoming ice*

Now footsteps on shingle. Make of it what you will. Sea-birds roost
on the breakwaters, accustomed, of course, to twilight.
The spirit-lamp in that house on the headland could easily fall
    and spill
and the fire burn all night. Some time later, a subtle ghost,
yourself in memory perhaps, might well set foot
up there amid clinker and smoke, the whole place silent and still
except you bring in the *tic* of cooling timbers, and then the birds
    in flight.

*

Now chains through gravel. Make of it what you will.

Fire: *a party at the world's end*

Scorched earth, the final notes or else the first,
bells and drums at the sea's edge where they've built
bonfires against the last and worst
of the day, deep dusk overlapping
the shoreline, treeline, rockfall, hills as they melt
in secret bowls of blue, the wavetops folding
fire on fire . . . and just where music and sea are lost
to one another, where nothing can be seen and nothing felt,
they dance like broken things, unstrung and calling.

They are drinking the last of the wine having drunk
the last of the water. Something came out of the sea
slow and blind; they spiked it on a spit
and ate it bare-handed. There was nothing of comfort or blame.

And still the great storms making landfall, the ice-walls shelving,
going under, forests emptying into silence, chaos out of flame,
through veils of smoke and smut the blank
stare of angels as they tread the air, as they ransack the sublime.

    *

NOTEBOOK: *Vesica piscis; solar eclipse; a leaf
from the Yggdrasil; IXΘYΣ; vulva of the goddess;
perfect completion; the end of everything.*

    *

Not least the ranks of the godly, incense and prayer
winding into the smoke; not least the demagogues, their rant
shrill on the wind then lost; not least the brothers in arms
whose ghosts walk with them; not least the dog-
soldiers of the rich list leaving a chain of zeros on the air . . .

[55]

Those few on the tideline are simply filling dreams
they knew they were bound to have: the rag-
ends, flashbacks, jump-cuts, subliminals, the scant
soundscape, the blinding sunsets, a vast machine
thrown hard into reverse: flywheels stripping the cogs,
then fault-lines, landslip, glass dominoes folding their silver
along the city skyline, what might be a stampede over bare
earth or else tectonic wrench or white-water or the gut-roar
of voices in terror rising, dying; and all that fever
returned by them in song: echoes from somewhere in-between.

*

It burns. Whole libraries on an updraught. Cascade of wings.
Substructure meltdown. What the night-sky brings.
Ashfall. Stars failing, fading. Unbreathable crosswinds.
Torrent of wildfire. No maps, no destinations.

They walk in carrying gismos, pillows, photos, whatever first
came to hand and stand
silent a moment, then line up with the rest.

*

NOTEBOOK: *(Docetic text) – this unadorned account*
of Christ the Trickster walking on coals: he comes
towards them, untouched, striding above the pain.

*

Slow march to the self-same music, each soon lost in the smoke
as if that long line were passing at my back, as if the smoke
rose from these unread books, this scrap and chaff, as if the smoke
might carry that far and all this lumber, like them, be lost in the smoke.

A rising night-wind now, the fire quickens, a vixen calls
close by. That pulse in the air is the sudden onrush of souls.

                *

A flight of stairs that spirals to a pinpoint, a door
that opens onto black rain, flocks of birds
that stream to a wall of flame and shrivel in flight: those dreams
were stock-in-trade to the spaewife and the seer,
a gralloched hare, mirror-gazing, knucklebones
thrown down on a magic square to make each time the same
pattern or the pattern reversed, which showed no less in the cards
not of prophecy but enlightenment . . . and there it was: the trek
to the sea under thin white skies, the firestorm at their backs,
their burdens, their weeping cries, the way the line
would lean as if for emphasis into a driven pall
of dust and dreck, while those who'd found the path
to the shore dance in the firelight, drink what they looted, fall
fast on one another, crowing, wretched with need,
as if love were always loss, as if flesh might soon be food.

                *

NOTEBOOK: *(Kafka: Sel. György Kurtág)*
Nevermore will you return
to the cities; nevermore
will the great bell sound above you.

*

As I turn out the last of it, the framework shifts and falls; a bright
rush of embers goes up; these letters (especially these)
fly to the centre and catch; nothing left to lose
(the circle closed) nothing left to do but see out the night.

*

Music against the dragback of the sea, the madcap roar
of their voices lifting into the wind, the endless
chorus of pain from the thousand thousand walking the wilderness,
rubble of clinker, tarmacadam rivers, pathways of broken glass,
a forest of dead wood holding its heat, the fire so fierce at the core
that it keeps a deep white silence, evidence of the flaw
that clouds the human heart and resolves to emptiness.

*

NOTEBOOK: *(Layard, et al) The prophet-hare*
looks out wide-eyed from the very seat of the blaze . . .

*

It breaks and reforms: patterns unpick, the dance
dips and spills, a churn of heads and arms, spin-daze
of ecstasy, a deadweight on the air

which is augury, which is judgment, which is fire feeding fire.

[58]

Icefield

A place of ice over ice, of white over white
and beauty in absences. There was a time when the only sound
was the wind calling its ghosts, when the skyline was set

clean as a scar on glass, when your heartbeat slowed
with the cold, when your dreams brought in a white bird
on a white sky and music that could only be heard

from time to time on the other side of night.
Now the horizon's a smudge; now there's a terrible weight
in the air and a stain cut hard and deep in the permafrost.

Breakage and slippage; the rumble of some vast
machine cranking its pistons, of everything on the slide;
and the water rising fast, and the music lost.

M.A.D. 1971 (Rat-run)

It will be the rat, he told her, the rat that first emerges from the crud
and crap after the infinite rapture of the megaton strike, its head
slick with what it burrowed through, what fell, what kept it fed.

You and I will close and fuse, bone seared to bone, flesh folded in.
Our silhouette will print the wall, one subterfuge, one skin.
Joined as never before, but joined, as we would have wished, in sin.

*

There were men in the seas of the moon. The great hare lay dead.
What they seemed to speak were broken lines of some unbroken code.
What they seemed to hear was the voice of God howling in the void.

Earth was a rolling abstract, its blue-white trappings dense
in darkness. They named it *terra nullius*. They were drenched
in starlight, dead light. They scuffed the dust as they danced.

*

It's nine, he told her, can you see? Nine, which multiplied
by any number reduces again to nine – vows of the woodland bride,
choirs of angels, fleshly portals, nine versions of the road

to Gethsemane . . . Bad luck, of course, to dream in nines
but it can only have been in sleep that I saw them, rat-clones
in a whirlwind of ash, the city burn-out, the broken stones.

Pain

Let's say a gallery. Let's say ill weather. Let's say you've moved
from *L'Arbre de Fluides* to *La Fenêtre*. Let's say you're not Marie,
not one of the *Corps de Dame*. Let's say you've been better loved.
Let's say that one of these, for sure, is what you came to see.

*

Red and black. Heart and hand. Sand and salt. You make a note.
The colours a crosshatch. The body parts a badge. The minerals
    a potion.
The city is sunstruck and pitiless. Dog packs in the backstreets.
    And what
will come of white nights, journeys never taken, this sorry waste
    of passion?

*

Pain of what's incurable, pain of what's broken, pain of the
    missing limb,
of something suddenly kicking in: little ratchety flywheel snug
to the heart, of what's beginning, even now, to swarm
in the blood, of what comes back, of what will settle, soon enough,
    and snag.

*

You wake from a dream where people go by rote. The clocks are set
one at the right time, one to fool the Devil. The penitents come out
hooded and gowned in holy white to flog themselves down the street.
The rhythm of that scourging, their dumbness, the rack of bloodied
    feet.

*

If not a cellar, an attic. If not walls of stone, then walls of glass.
Now music from another room, the way it hangs in air,
the way light scintillates, the way mirrors will pass
an image between them: raw scorch beneath the skin, that lidless
    stare.

*

Here, something is eating something. Here, a woman screams
into the face of another. Here, someone is banging someone. Here,
the women are reversed, or else they were never women except
    in dreams.
There's room after room of it; go as you will: as often, as deep, as far.

*

Pain of remembrance, pain of possession, pain of the last look back.
A lock without a door; a voiceless choir. There are stories that govern
    this:
the father's return, the lovers who walked a year in each other's tracks
lost and appalled, the one-time touch, the fearful consequence of
    bliss.

*

The serial wife, that blonde recidivist . . . Memories of the city,
camera obscura, roofscape and streetplan, her contour slipping past
noiseless and matt-black. Love as hunger, improvisations of pity,
the all-or-nothing of the day-to-day: return to that if you must.

*

A train at midnight stalled between nothing and nowhere; from here
  you get
faces at windows, dead silence, tonnage, a line of leafless trees
marking the dim perimeter. Fixity like this depends on loss and regret:
freeze-frame on the unshed tear; still life with arum lily and hourglass.

*

Shadow-play on doorways and stairways – merge with this, you'll fit
as everyone fits, duck or hare, beauty or hag, some other self
sidling in, eager for news of you, eager to make the cut.
Walk in and out of the light. Now pause. There's your half-and-half.

*

Pain in birdsong, pain in rough weather, pain in the sound of the sea,
the air thick with contagion, windborne, isobars of the fever-chart,
skim on rivers, spoilage and spillage, gutter-run . . . In this cold simile
of God's clean sweep, first to fall is the wise child, hand on heart.

*

As if someone might turn, lost and lost again, trying to take a fix
on stars for a compass point. As if the sun might rise
in a place of trackless dust. As if they might be tricks
of the light: the way on, the way back, and the day itself a disguise.

*

The perfect lie is a sculptural thing, dense and touchable. The
    perfect lie
has a steady inner light. The perfect lie goes hand in hand with you
to the point of no return. There's a voice in the room, half-heard
    (don't try
to guess at that) and out in the street wild music from which you take
    your cue.

        *

A working model of the fall from grace, a back-lit auto-da-fé, the last
of the species, caught and caged. It's a raree show: Iscariot's fallen tear,
the Devil's burlesque, something both fur and fin . . . and then the rest
one by one as the handle's cranked – what you both love and fear.

        *

Pain as quittance, pain as touchstone, pain as a last resort.
Imagine some long-limbed creature hauled by its hocks to be flayed,
the knife set right to the whetstone, music to work by, a caught
breath as the moment unpicks between flesh and blade.

Acknowledgements and Notes

'Bowland Beth': commissioned for *The Sparrowhawk's Lament* by David Cobham, published by Princeton University Press. First UK publication: *New Statesman*. The hen harrier is on the verge of extinction in England thanks to systematic, gleeful, illegal persecution: hen harriers take grouse. Bowland Beth was killed before she could breed.

'Tinnitus': the initial poem in this sequence was commissioned for *Signs and Humours*, edited by Lavinia Greenlaw, published by Calouste Gulbenkian Foundation. This affliction is much like one of the trials of Job: not so much a condition, more a test. It is generally thought to be a ringing in the ears – and it most often is – but it's more than that. I give three versions; there are many more. It overplays music; it crowds out thought; it is relentless; there is no defence. It might be the uninterpretable voices of angels.

'Effaced': commissioned for *Their Colours and Their Forms*, edited by Carol McKay and John Strachan, published by Art Editions North and the Wordsworth Trust. Subsequently published in *Poem*, edited by Fiona Sampson, and, later, in the *Poetry London Anthology*, edited by Ahren Warner.

'Armistice': commissioned for *1914: Poetry Remembers*, edited by Carol Ann Duffy, published by Faber & Faber.

'Trickster Christ': commissioned for *Poetry Ireland Review*, edited by John F. Deane.

'Dive': commissioned for an exhibition at the Sydney Opera House. Photographic images by Simon Harsent. UK publication: *New Statesman*.

'Songs from the Same Earth' was a Royal Philharmonic Society/ Britten-Pears Foundation commission to celebrate the centenary of the birth of Benjamin Britten and the bicentenary of the foundation of the Royal Philharmonic Society. The poems were set to music by Harrison Birtwistle and the piece first performed at the Aldeburgh Festival 2013. The sequence was published as a Rack Press pamphlet in 2013.

'Icefield': one of three poems commissioned by the Leo Burnett Agency for the World Wide Fund for Nature Australia campaign and produced as poster poems. Photographic images by Simon Harsent. The poems were broadcast on ABC. UK publication: *Poetry Review*.

'M.A.D. 1971 (Rat-run)': commissioned for *Jubilee Lines*, edited by Carol Ann Duffy, published by Faber & Faber. Each poet commissioned for *Jubilee Lines* was given a year during the Queen's reign as his or her subject. My given year brought two things to mind: the Apollo 15 moon landing and the fact that we were, at that time, in the thick of the Cold War. M.A.D. is an acronym for mutually assured destruction: the means by which (it was claimed) the standoff between East and West was maintained. I also saw that the digits of 1971, if added, reduce to nine. Nine is a magical number. The product of any number multiplied by nine will, in the same way, reduce to nine. And the rat is ineradicable.

'Pain': *L'Arbre de Fluides* is a painting by Jean Dubuffet: one of the *Corps de Dames* series. *La Fenêtre* is a painting by Pierre Bonnard.

Other poems appeared in *Edinburgh Review*, *London Review of Books*, *New Humanist*, *New Statesman*, *Poem*, *Poetry* (USA), *Poetry London* and *Poetry Review*.